NEW MEXICO
A TO Z

by
DOROTHY
HINES WEAVER

Illustrated by
KAY
WACKER

NORTHLAND PUBLISHING

The illustrations were done in dyes and color pencils on illustration board
The text type was set in Stempel Garamond
The display type was set in Copperplate
Composed in the United States of America
Edited by Stephanie Morrison
Production supervised by Lisa Brownfield

Manufactured in Hong Kong by Wing King Tong.

FIRST IMPRESSION
ISBN 0-87358-636-0

Library of Congress Catalog Card Number 95-41614
Library of Congress Cataloging-in-Publication Data
Weaver, Dorothy Hines.
New Mexico A to Z / by Dorothy Hines Weaver ;
illustrated by Kay Wacker.
p.   cm.
Summary: Presents fascinating facts about New Mexico, representing
each letter of the alphabet, from aerial attraction above
Albuquerque to the Zuni River.
ISBN 0-87358-636-0
1. New Mexico—Juvenile literature. 2. English language—
Alphabet—Juvenile literature. [1. New Mexico. 2. Alphabet.]
I. Wacker, Kay, ill. II. Title.
F796.3.W43 1996
978.9—dc20   95-41614

0542/7.5M/3-96

With thanks to the Lord for
His countless blessings.

Aerial attraction above Albuquerque

Aa

Black bear browsing in Bandelier

Bb

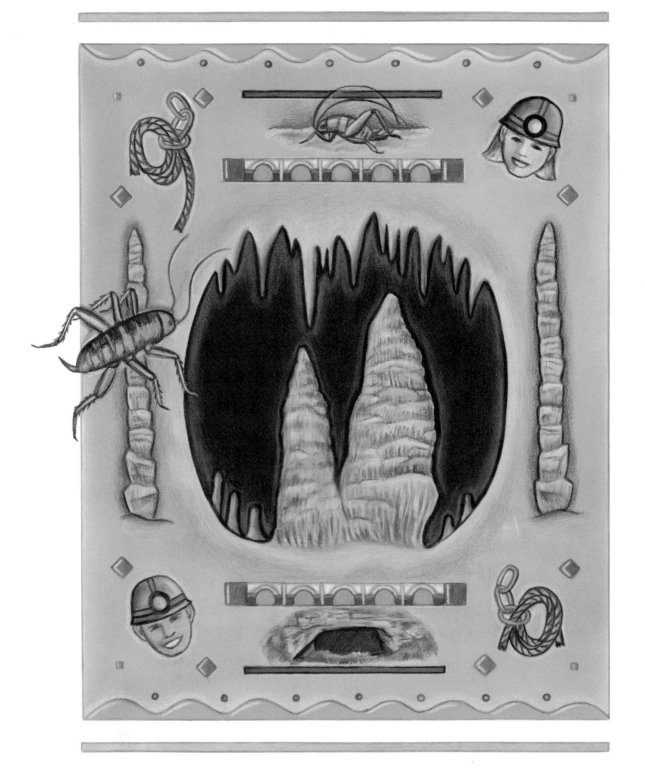

Cave cricket crawling in Carlsbad Caverns

Cc

Ducks dash during Deming race

Dd

Elk emerging at El Malpais

Ee

Fiestas focusing on family fun

Groundsel gracing the Gila Wilderness

Gg

Hoedown happening at Hobbs

Hh

Indian paintbrush illuminating Isleta

Ii

Junco jetting by Jemez

Jj

Kiva kept up in Kuaua

Kk

Luminarias line lighted lodgings

Ll

Mountain lion making tracks on Manzano Mountains

Mm

Nutcracker nesting near Navajo Lake

Nn

Oriole observing Oasis State Park

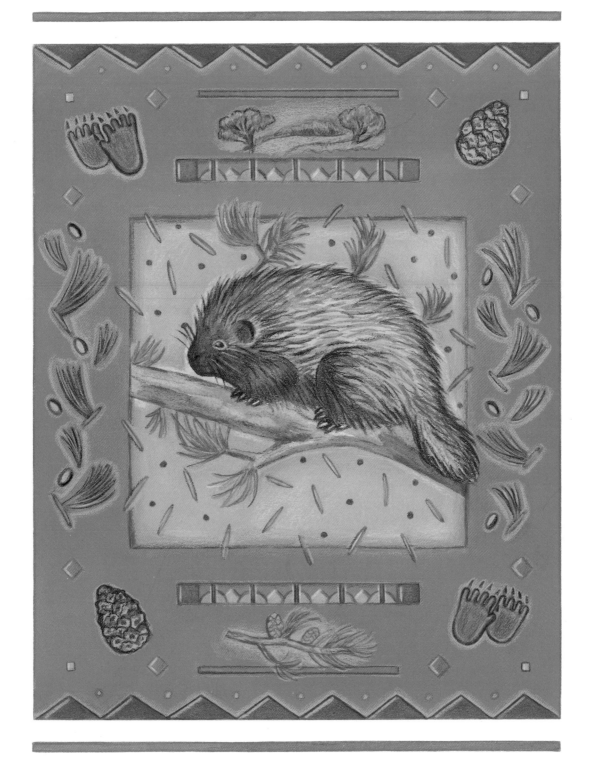

Porcupine perched in a piñon pine

Pp

Queen's Crown quivering by Quemado

Rafters running the Río Grande

Skiers skimming Santa Fe slopes

Ss

Tourists taking in Taos treasures

Tt

Urosaurus undulating by underbrush

Uu

Vulture viewing volcano vistas

Winds whirling White Sands

Ww

Xylosma exhibited in xeriscape

Xx

Yucca moth in Yankee Canyon

Zone-tail zooming by Zuni River

Zz

New Mexico is called the Land of Enchantment. It became our forty-seventh state on January 6, 1912. New Mexico was named by Spanish explorers who were searching for gold. The state flag displays the ancient sun symbol of the Zia Pueblo. The state colors are red and yellow. The state motto Crescit Eundo is Latin for "It grows as it goes."

aerial attraction   The Sandia Peak Tram is the world's longest tramway. It is located near Albuquerque and it affords spectacular panoramic views as it rises to the top of 10,400-foot Sandia Peak.

Albuquerque   New Mexico's largest city is an important trade and transportation center. Historic Old Town Albuquerque is known for enjoyable shopping, dining and sightseeing.

Bandelier   Bandelier National Monument, located west of Santa Fe, contains colorful canyons, forested mesas, and ancient ruins. There are many trails through its scenic and rugged back country.

black bear   New Mexico's state mammal can run as fast as thirty miles per hour and is a good tree climber and swimmer. This large bear feeds on almost everything and hibernates in a den for several months each winter.

Carlsbad Caverns   This national park in southeastern New Mexico has huge underground limestone caves and chambers with fantastic rock formations. Visitors can tour the fascinating connected caverns.

cave crickets   These nocturnal insects live in caves, crawling on the walls and floors. They can even walk upside down on the ceilings.

Deming   The Great American Duck Race is held each August in Deming in southwestern New Mexico. Deming boasts of its mild seasons and of being the chili capital of the world.

elk   This large member of the deer family has huge, spreading antlers. Elk usually live in herds and are often seen in the open or on mountain meadows, foothills, and plains. They graze on grasses, herbs, and woody vegetation.

El Malpais   El Malpais (ell-mal-pie-EES) means badlands in Spanish. This national monument in northwestern New Mexico features a variety of landscape—mesas, mountain ranges, sandstone formations, ancient cinder caves, and lava flows. It includes a large scenic wilderness area.

fiestas   Gala celebrations and colorful festivals commemorate special events. Balloon fiestas and rallies are held throughout New Mexico.

Gila Wilderness   This vast area is part of Gila (HE-la) National Forest in southwestern New Mexico. In 1924 it became the nation's first forest wilderness area. There are hundreds of miles of trails in the Gila.

groundsel   This bushy plant belongs to the sunflower family. Its flowers form seeds with white woolly hairs. Groundsel is common in the Gila Wilderness.

Hobbs   This thriving city is located in the ranch and oil country of southeastern New Mexico. Hobbs Hoedown Days are held annually. A yearly Hang Gliding Meet is also held in Hobbs; its dry thermals make for ideal soaring conditions.

hoedown   A hoedown is a community festival or party with lively dancing and celebrations.

Indian paintbrush   This colorful plant of the snapdragon family has bright bracts or leaves while the flowers are small and inconspicuous. It usually grows in clumps up to three feet tall.

Isleta   The Isleta (iss-LAY-täh) Indian Reservation, south of Albuquerque, extends into grassy plains and timbered mountains. The Isleta Pueblo is one of the Southwest's largest pueblos. Its St. Augustine Church includes portions of the original mission church built in 1626.

Jemez   The rugged Jemez (HAY-mess) Mountain Complex, in northwestern New Mexico, includes Jemez Falls. Some other Jemez attractions are: the large Jemez Pueblo, Jemez Canyon Dam and Lake, and Jemez State Monument with its impressive ruins that were the original home of the Jemez Indians.

junco   The dark-eyed junco is a ground-dwelling bird that likes woodlands and clearings. It feeds on berries, seeds, and insects.

kiva   The sunken religious ceremonial kiva (KEE-va) chamber was an important part of ancient pueblos—communal villages that were built of adobe or stone.

Kuaua   The Kuaua (koo-AH-wa) Pueblo kiva in Coronado State Monument has been restored and partially reconstructed. Ancient ceremonial paintings and murals were uncovered and are preserved there.

luminarias   Small votive candles are placed in sand-filled paper bags and lit for decoration. Luminarias are also known as farolitos and are a New Mexican tradition, especially at Christmas.

Manzano Mountains   Manzano Mountains State Park is located in the wooded foothills of the Manzano Mountains in central New Mexico. Early settlers planted apple orchards in the area. Manzano means "apple tree" in Spanish.

mountain lion   This large powerful cat found in the Southwest is a great traveler and a good climber. It can jump twenty to thirty feet. Its mating call is a piercing scream.

Navajo Lake   This lake in northwestern New Mexico is surrounded by three developed recreational areas—Pine River, Sims Mesa, and San Juan River. Navajo Lake areas feature boating, waterskiing, and fishing.

nutcracker   Clark's nutcracker pecks at cones to pry out the seeds. This industrious bird stores the seeds in pouches under its tongue until it buries them in the ground.

Oasis State Park   This lovely park in central eastern New Mexico, southwest of Clovis, is known for its sand dunes and large shade trees. There are picnic and camping sites in the area and also a fishing lake.

oriole   Bullock's oriole is a brightly colored bird with a piping whistled song. It dwells in desert trees and in woodlands. Its deep baglike nest can be seen hanging down from a limb or branch.

piñon pine   The state tree of New Mexico is a small, slow-growing evergreen. Its seeds—piñon nuts—are edible.

porcupine   This quilled animal lives in forest and brushy areas of the Southwest. It climbs well, spending time in trees. It eats buds, berries, leaves, twigs, bark, and the seeds of piñon pine.

Queen's Crown   This wildflower displays small clusters of tiny flowers and can be seen along streamsides and on rocky outcrops in mountain areas.

Quemado   The scenic Quemado Lake Recreation Area is in the northern part of the Gila National Forest, south of Quemado, New Mexico. Attractions include camping, boating, hiking, and wildlife viewing.

Río Grande   New Mexico's most important waterway runs through the center of the state from north to south. Río Grande means "great river" in Spanish. Rafters like to challenge the rapids of the Río Grande.

Santa Fe   The oldest capital city in the nation, Santa Fe was settled in the early 1600s. Points of interest include the Plaza with its gift shops and galleries, and the historic Spanish Palace of the Governors. The Santa Fe Ski Area affords fine downhill skiing.

Taos   This colorful town welcomes visitors to explore interesting plaza galleries, bookstores, and shops. Locally crafted items include paintings, sculpture, jewelry, Indian baskets, and weavings. Taos Ski Valley also attracts vacationers.

urosaurus   Tree lizards can be seen moving or undulating on rocks or in trees—sometimes even hanging head down. This small reptile is most active mornings and late afternoons, often hiding under shrubs or bushes. Its range includes New Mexico.

volcano vistas   Capulin (Cah-poo-LEEN) Volcano National Monument affords magnificent views from the trail that encircles Crater Rim. The inside of the volcano can be seen by walking on a self-guiding trail to the bottom of the crater.

vulture   Turkey vultures, sometimes called buzzards, are large birds of prey that can soar and glide gracefully.

White Sands   This unique national monument has the world's largest gypsum dune fields and they are always changing. Winds can whip the glistening white sands into different wavelike patterns.

xeriscape   This type of landscape conserves water and displays the natural beauty of the desert.

xylosma   Low water-use plants are used in desert landscaping. Xylosma shrubs have glossy leaves, insignificant green flowers and greenish-to-red berries.

Yankee Canyon   This beautiful canyon area is located east of Raton near Sugarite (shoog-ar-EET) Canyon State Park, a forested mountain park on the northern border with Colorado.

yucca moth   Small night-flying moths depend on the yucca (YUH-ka) plant for food while the yucca depends on the yucca moth to pollinate its flowers. There are many yucca species that grow in the Southwest. The soaptree yucca's blossom is the New Mexico state flower.

zone-tail   The zone-tailed hawk has long, slender wings and likes flying over canyons and rivers.

Zuni River   This quiet river in western New Mexico flows through the colorful Zuni mountains, the Zuni Indian Reservation, and past the large Zuni Pueblo.

DOROTHY HINES WEAVER AND KAY WACKER, the mother-daughter team that wrote and illustrated Northland's *Arizona A to Z,* have lived in Arizona for more than twenty years.

DOROTHY received her B.S. in Education from the University of Nebraska at Omaha and is a former elementary teacher and school librarian. She has three daughters and four grandchildren. Dorothy and her oldest daughter, Kay, traveled throughout New Mexico together to research this book.

KAY received her B.F.A. with an emphasis in illustration from Northern Arizona University and has a background in graphic design. She has worked as an illustrator for the past nine years and enjoys illustrating children's books because it allows her the flexibility to spend time with her son, Trent, who is five, and daughter, Kara, three. Working with her mom, she says, makes a project more meaningful to her.

David Shough